Charmed
by Moda Bake Shop

A Dozen Delightful Charm Pack Quilts

Compiled by Lissa Alexander

Martingale
Create with Confidence

Charmed by Moda Bake Shop: A Dozen Delightful
Charm Pack Quilts
© 2022 by Martingale & Company®

Martingale®
18939 120th Ave. NE, Ste. 101
Bothell, WA 98011-9511 USA
ShopMartingale.com

Printed in the United States of America
27 26 25 24 23 22   8 7 6 5 4 3 2 1

Library of Congress Cataloging-in-Publication Data is
available upon request.

ISBN: 978-1-68356-217-7

MISSION STATEMENT

We empower makers who use fabric and yarn
to make life more enjoyable.

CREDITS

**PRESIDENT AND
CHIEF VISIONARY OFFICER**
Jennifer Erbe Keltner

CONTENT DIRECTOR
Karen Costello Soltys

DESIGN MANAGER
Adrienne Smitke

TECHNICAL EDITOR
Nancy Mahoney

PRODUCTION MANAGER
Regina Girard

COPY EDITOR
Melissa Bryan

COVER DESIGNER
Mia Mar

ILLUSTRATOR
Sandy Loi

PHOTOGRAPHERS
Adam Albright
Brent Kanet

SPECIAL THANKS
*Photography for this book was taken at
the homes of Kristen Yanasak in Everett, Washington,
and Lianne Anderson in Arlington, Washington.*

Contents

Introduction

Charmed: ADJECTIVE. *Enamored, captivated, enchanted, fascinated.*

Don't those words capture the sentiments of exceptional quilts that give us "all the feels"?

Did you know Charm Packs are the very first precut fabrics that Moda offered more than 15 years ago? And these packs of precut 5" squares are just as captivating and fascinating as ever to quilters everywhere! Why? Because you get 42 squares, at least one of each print in a fabric collection, giving you a wide variety of fabrics for an affordable price. Looking to build a scrappy stash? Charm Packs to the rescue! And, because the fabrics in a Charm Pack are all from the same fabric collection, you know they'll blend together beautifully.

But even knowing the fabrics will work together doesn't mean you're not also on the lookout for patterns written for using Charm Packs. Enter the Moda Bake Shop designers.

With this book, these talented quilt designers share patterns for a dozen original quilts, each perfect for using one or more Charm Packs—whether they are ones you've been saving in your stash, or you can't wait buy a brand-new Charm Pack or two. From the adorable little row sampler shown on the front cover to a fool-the-eye Shoo Fly (page 65) to a retro-style Cobblestones quilt (page 7), the toughest part will be choosing which quilt to make first. But whichever you choose, your quilt is sure to be captivating. You'll be charmed, I'm sure!

~ Lissa

Cobblestones

ANNE WIENS

Cheerful primary colors set a delightful tone for Anne's design, which features positive-negative motifs. This pattern is easier than it looks, as the secondary design emerges organically when the blocks are set together in rows. The design also breaks right into the outer border for a fun finish.

FINISHED QUILT: 56½" × 68½"
FINISHED BLOCK: 12" × 12"

Materials

Yardage is based on 42"-wide fabric. A Moda Fabrics charm pack contains 42 squares, 5" × 5". Anne used 30's Playthings by Chole's Closet for Moda Fabrics.

○ 4 matching charm packs *OR* 150 squares, 5" × 5", of assorted prints for blocks and border*

○ 2¼ yards of white solid for blocks and border

○ 1 yard of navy print for border

○ ⅝ yard of yellow print for binding

○ 3½ yards of fabric for backing

○ 63" × 75" piece of batting

*You can substitute 1 Moda Layer Cake for the 4 matching charm packs if desired. Cut each Layer Cake square into 4 squares, 5" × 5".

Plan Ahead

Plan your fabric pairings before cutting the 5" squares. For each of the 20 blocks, choose four matching squares and label them as fabric A. Select one square from a contrasting print and label it as fabric B. Then select one square for the center of the block and label it as fabric C. Repeat to make 20 sets of fabric A–C squares. Select 30 squares for the block corners and label them as fabric D.

Cutting

All measurements include ¼" seam allowances. Before cutting, see "Plan Ahead," above, to label the A–D squares.

From *each* of the fabric A squares, cut:
1 square, 4½" × 4½" (80 total)

From *each* of the fabric B squares, cut:
4 squares, 2½" × 2½" (80 total)

From *each* of the fabric C squares, cut:
1 square, 4½" × 4½" (20 total)

From *each* of the fabric D squares, cut:
4 squares, 2½" × 2½" (120 total)

From the white solid, cut:
28 strips, 2½" × 42"; crosscut into:
- 80 pieces, 2½" × 4½"
- 276 squares, 2½" × 2½"

From the navy print, cut:
7 strips, 4½" × 42"; crosscut into:
- 36 pieces, 4½" × 6½"
- 4 squares, 4½" × 4½"

From the yellow print, cut:
7 strips, 2½" × 42"

Making the Blocks

Instructions are for making one block. Repeat to make a total of 20 blocks. Press seam allowances in the directions indicated by the arrows.

1 Join a B square and a white square. Sew a white piece to one side as shown. Make four matching corner units measuring 4½" square, including seam allowances.

Make 4 units,
4½" × 4½".

2 Draw a diagonal line from corner to corner on the wrong side of eight white squares. Place a marked square on one corner of an A square, right sides together. Sew on the marked line. Trim the excess corner fabric ¼" from the stitched line. Place a marked square on an adjacent corner of the A square. Sew and trim as before. Make four matching side units measuring 4½" square, including seam allowances.

Make 4 units,
4½" × 4½".

Charmed by Moda Bake Shop

3 Lay out the four corner units, four side units, and one C square in three rows, rotating the units as shown. Sew the pieces into rows and then join the rows. Repeat to make 20 blocks measuring 12½" square, including seam allowances.

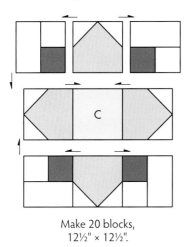

Make 20 blocks,
12½" × 12½".

Assembling the Quilt Top

1 Draw a diagonal line from corner to corner on the wrong side of the remaining white squares. Place a marked square on the upper-right corner of a navy piece, right sides together. Sew on the marked line. Trim the excess corner fabric ¼" from the stitched line. Make 18 units measuring 4½" × 6½", including seam allowances. Place a marked square on the upper-left corner of a navy piece, right sides together. Sew and trim as before to make 18 mirror-image units.

 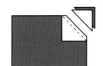

Make 18 of each unit,
4½" × 6½".

2 Join one unit and one mirror-image unit to make a border unit. Make 18 units measuring 4½" × 12½", including seam allowances.

Make 18 border units,
4½" × 12½".

3 Draw a diagonal line from corner to corner on the wrong side of the D squares.

4 Before assembling the quilt top, lay out the blocks on a design wall in five rows of four blocks each as shown in the quilt layout. This allows you to plan the fabrics used in the corner triangles of each block and adjacent border unit. Add the border units around the outer edges of the blocks and place a navy square in each corner of the border.

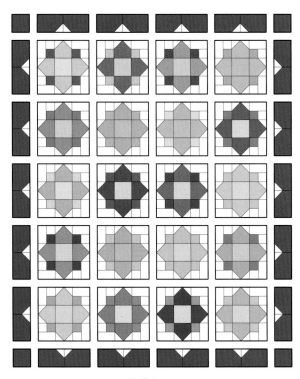

Quilt layout

5 Pin a D square to each block intersection and each intersection of blocks and corresponding border units. Where four D squares meet, they should all be the same fabric.

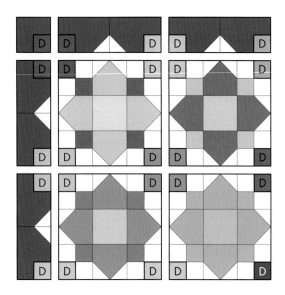

6 For each block, place the marked squares on the corners of the block, right sides together, and making sure the marked squares are in the correct position. Sew on the marked lines. Trim the excess corner fabric ¼" from the stitched lines. Return each block to its correct position on the design wall.

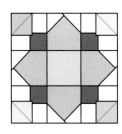 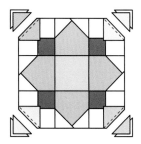

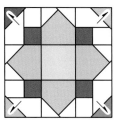

Make 20 blocks,
12½" × 12½".

Designed by Anne Wiens; quilted by Doris Koontz.

See more from Anne at SweetgrassDesigns.wordpress.com.

7 Repeat step 6 for each border unit. Return each unit to its correct position on the design wall.

 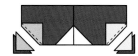

Make 18 border units,
4½" × 12½".

8 Place a marked square on each navy square. Sew and trim as before. Return each square to its correct position on the design wall.

Make 4 units,
4½" × 4½".

9 Referring to the quilt assembly diagram below, sew the pieces into rows and then join the rows. The quilt top should measure 56½" × 68½".

Finishing the Quilt

For more details on any finishing steps, visit ShopMartingale.com/HowtoQuilt for free downloadable information.

1 Because the quilt border has many seams that could open up, stitch around the perimeter of the quilt top, ⅛" from the outer edges, to lock the seams in place before quilting.

2 Layer the quilt top with batting and backing; baste the layers together.

3 Quilt by hand or machine. Anne's quilt is machine quilted with an allover design of flowers and leaves.

4 Use the yellow 2½"-wide strips to make double-fold binding. Attach the binding to the quilt.

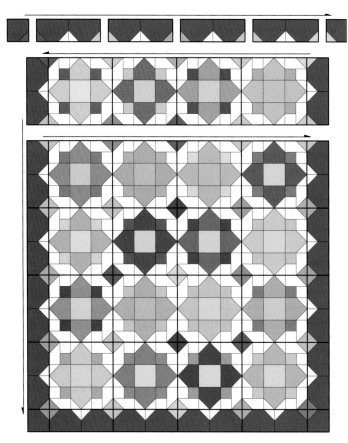

Quilt assembly

N.S.E.W.

LISA JO GIRODAT

Thank goodness for navigation apps on our phones, because Lisa Jo says she can get lost simply driving to a family member's home. Thus, the inspiration for this quilt, aptly named N.S.E.W. A quarter turn of a block in alternating columns creates a fun pattern that appears to be pointing north, south, east, and west.

FINISHED QUILT: 65½" × 65½"
FINISHED BLOCK: 12" × 12"

Materials

Yardage is based on 42"-wide fabric. A Moda Fabrics charm pack contains 42 squares, 5" × 5". Lisa Jo used Midnight in the Garden by Sweetfire Road for Moda Fabrics.

- 2 charm packs OR 75 squares, 5" × 5", of assorted prints for blocks
- 3 yards of gray solid for blocks
- ¾ yard of pink print for border
- ⅝ yard of black print for binding
- 4 yards of fabric for backing
- 72" × 72" piece of batting

Cutting

All measurements include ¼" seam allowances.

From *each of 25* assorted print squares, cut:
4 squares, 2½" × 2½" (100 total)

From the gray solid, cut:
7 strips, 5" × 42"; crosscut into 50 squares, 5" × 5"
18 strips, 2½" × 42"; crosscut into:
- 25 strips, 2½" × 12½"
- 100 pieces, 2½" × 3½"

13 strips, 1½" × 42"; crosscut into 50 strips,
    1½" × 8½"

From the pink print, cut:
7 strips, 3" × 42"

From the black print, cut:
7 strips, 2½" × 42"

Making the Blocks

Press seam allowances in the directions indicated
by the arrows.

1 Draw a diagonal line from corner to corner
on the wrong side of the gray 5" squares. Layer
a marked square on a print 5" square, right sides
together. Sew ¼" from both sides of the drawn line.
Cut the unit apart on the marked line. Make 100
half-square-triangle units and trim them to 4½"
square, including seam allowances.

Make 100 units.

2 Join two matching half-square-triangle units
as shown. Sew a gray 1½" × 8½" strip to the
top edge. Make 50 units measuring 5½" × 8½",
including seam allowances.

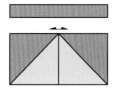 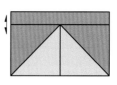

Make 50 units,
5½" × 8½".

3 Join a print 2½" square and a gray 2½" × 3½"
piece. Make 25 sets of four matching units
that measure 2½" × 5½", including seam
allowances.

Make 25 sets of
4 matching units,
2½" × 5½".

4 Lay out four matching units from step 3, two
units from step 2, and one gray 2½" × 12½"
strip, noting the orientation of the triangle units.
Sew the units into rows. Sew the rows to opposite
sides of the gray strip to make a block. Make 25
blocks measuring 12½" square, including seam
allowances.

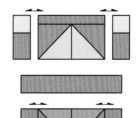 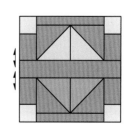

Make 25 blocks,
12½" × 12½".

Designed, pieced, and quilted by Lisa Jo Girodat.

Visit Lisa Jo on Instagram @neverlandstitches.

Assembling the Quilt Top

1 Referring to the quilt assembly diagram below, lay out the blocks in five rows of five blocks each, rotating every other block in each row as shown. Sew the blocks into rows and then join the rows. The quilt top should measure 60½" square, including seam allowances.

2 Join the pink 3"-wide strips end to end. From the pieced strip, cut two 65½"-long strips and two 60½"-long strips. Sew the shorter strips to the left and right sides of the quilt top. Sew the longer strips to the top and bottom edges. The quilt top should measure 65½" square.

Finishing the Quilt

For more details on any finishing steps, visit ShopMartingale.com/HowtoQuilt for free downloadable information.

1 Layer the quilt top with batting and backing; baste the layers together.

2 Quilt by hand or machine. Lisa Jo's quilt is machine quilted with an allover design of meandering lines and apple motifs.

3 Use the black 2½"-wide strips to make double-fold binding. Attach the binding to the quilt.

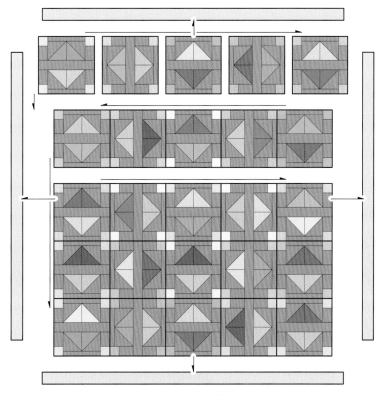

Quilt assembly

Pinwheel Wreaths

SUSAN VAUGHAN

Christmas is a favorite holiday for Susan, and one of her annual traditions is picking out a balsam fir wreath for her front door. The wreath brightens up her front porch and adds some holiday cheer to her neighborhood. This small charm pack–friendly quilt can be used as a wall hanging or table topper to bring that same festive and welcoming spirit into your home!

FINISHED QUILT: 49½" × 49½"
FINISHED BLOCK: 18" × 18"

Materials

Yardage is based on 42"-wide fabric. A Moda Fabrics charm pack contains 42 squares, 5" × 5". Susan used Christmas Stitched by Fig Tree & Co. for Moda Fabrics.

○ 2 charm packs OR:
  - 8 squares, 5" × 5", of assorted ivory prints for blocks
  - 16 squares, 5" × 5", of assorted red prints for blocks
  - 16 squares, 5" × 5", of assorted green prints for blocks
  - 8 squares, 5" × 5", of assorted tan prints for blocks
○ 2 yards of ivory solid for blocks, sashing, and inner border
○ ⅛ yard of red text print for sashing units
○ ½ yard of red pinecone print for outer border
○ ½ yard of green print for binding
○ 3⅛ yards of fabric for backing
○ 56" × 56" piece of batting

Cutting

All measurements include ¼" seam allowances.

From *each* of the assorted ivory print squares, cut:
1 square, 4" × 4" (8 total)

**From *4* of the assorted red print squares,
cut *2 matching sets* of:**
1 square, 4" × 4" (4 total)

**From *4* of the assorted green print squares,
cut *2 matching sets* of:**
1 square, 4" × 4" (4 total)

From the ivory solid, cut:
4 strips, 5" × 42"; crosscut into 32 squares, 5" × 5"
6 strips, 3½" × 42"; crosscut into:
- 16 pieces, 3½" × 6½"
- 32 squares, 3½" × 3½"

6 strips, 2½" × 42"; crosscut into 12 strips,
2½" × 18½"
1 strip, 2" × 42"; crosscut into 18 squares, 2" × 2"
5 strips, 1½" × 42"

From the red text print, cut:
1 strip, 2" × 42"; crosscut into 18 squares, 2" × 2"

From the red pinecone print, cut:
5 strips, 3" × 42"

From the green print for binding, cut:
6 strips, 2½" × 42"

Making the Pinwheel Units

Press seam allowances in the directions indicated
by the arrows.

1 Draw a diagonal line from corner to corner on
the wrong side of the ivory print 4" squares.
Layer a marked square on a red 4" square, right
sides together. Sew ¼" from both sides of the
drawn line. Cut the unit apart on the marked line.
Make two half-square-triangle units and trim them
to 3½" square, including seam allowances. Make

two sets of four matching red units. Use the green
4" squares and remaining marked ivory print
squares to make two sets of four matching green
triangle units.

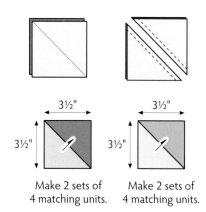

Make 2 sets of 4 matching units.   Make 2 sets of 4 matching units.

2 Lay out four matching red triangle units in two
rows, rotating the units to form a pinwheel.
Sew the units into rows and then join the rows to
make a large pinwheel unit. Make two red units
measuring 6½" square, including seam allowances.
Repeat using the green triangle units to make two
green units.

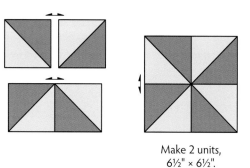

Make 2 units,
6½" × 6½".

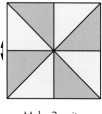

Make 2 units,
6½" × 6½".

Charmed by Moda Bake Shop

3 Draw a diagonal line from corner to corner in both directions to form an X on the wrong side of the ivory solid 5" squares. Layer a marked square on top of a red 5" square, right sides together. Sew ¼" from both sides of the drawn lines. Cut the units apart horizontally and vertically. Then cut the units apart on the drawn lines. Make eight red half-square-triangle units and trim them to 2" square, including seam allowances. Repeat to make 12 sets of eight matching red units. In the same way, use the marked squares and green 5" squares to make 12 sets of eight matching green units. Use the remaining marked squares and tan 5" squares to make eight sets of eight matching tan units.

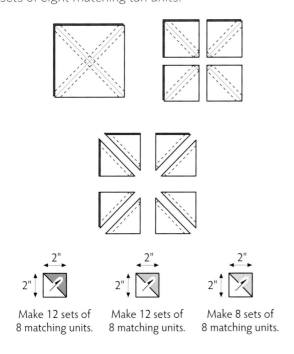

Make 12 sets of 8 matching units.   Make 12 sets of 8 matching units.   Make 8 sets of 8 matching units.

4 Lay out four matching red triangle units from step 3 in two rows, rotating the units to form a pinwheel. Sew the units into rows and then join

the rows to make a small pinwheel unit. Make 24 red units measuring 3½" square, including seam allowances. Repeat to make 24 green units and 16 tan units.

Make 24 units,
3½" × 3½".

Make 24 units,
3½" × 3½".   Make 16 units,
3½" × 3½".

Making the Blocks

1 Lay out one tan small pinwheel unit, one green small pinwheel unit, and two ivory solid 3½" squares in two rows as shown. Sew the pieces into rows and then join the rows. Make eight corner units measuring 6½" square, including seam allowances.

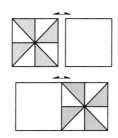 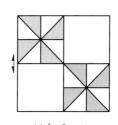

Make 8 units,
6½" × 6½".

2 Join two green small pinwheel units. Sew an ivory solid 3½" × 6½" piece to the bottom edge. Make eight side units measuring 6½" square, including seam allowances.

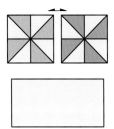 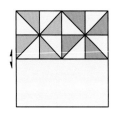

Make 8 units,
6½" × 6½".

3 Lay out four corner units, four side units, and one red large pinwheel unit in three rows, rotating the side units as shown. Sew the units into rows and then join the rows to make a block. Make two green blocks measuring 18½" square, including seam allowances.

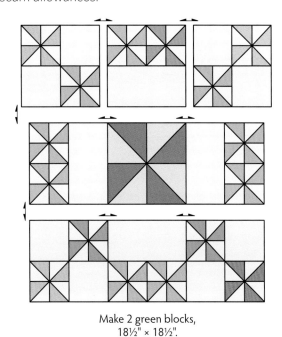

Make 2 green blocks,
18½" × 18½".

Pressing Matters

Pinwheels have long been favorite blocks for quilters, but they can lead to some challenges where the seams join in the middle. To make seams less bulky and to improve accuracy in piecing, press the seam allowances open. You may want to shorten the stitch length on your sewing machine to keep the seam allowances from coming undone along the edges.

4 Repeat steps 1–3 using the red small pinwheel units, remaining tan small pinwheel units, green large pinwheel units, and the remaining ivory solid 3½" × 6½" pieces and 3½" squares to make two red blocks measuring 18½" square, including seam allowances.

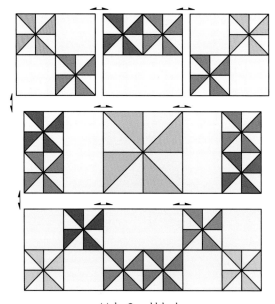

Make 2 red blocks,
18½" × 18½".

Charmed by Moda Bake Shop

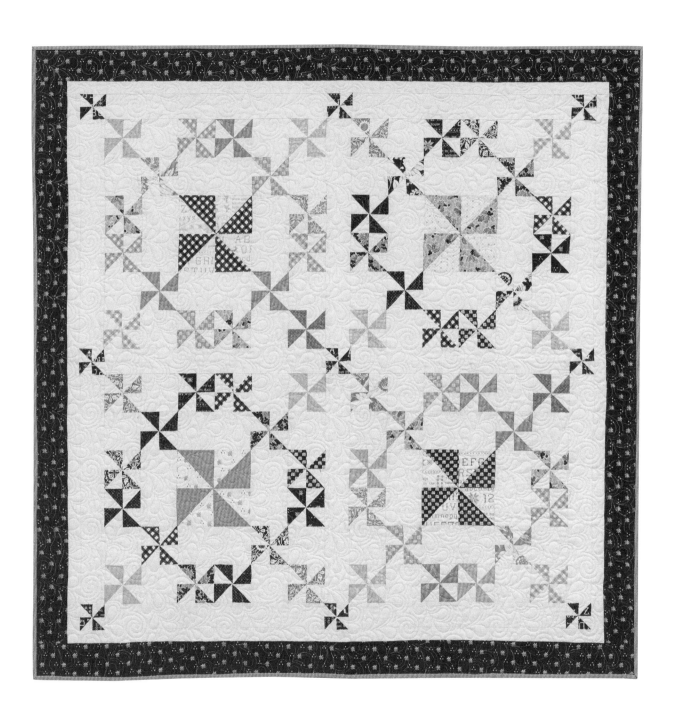

Designed, pieced, and quilted by Susan Vaughan.

Follow Susan's sewing adventures on Instagram @thefeltedpear.

Assembling the Quilt Top

1 Draw a diagonal line from corner to corner on the wrong side of the ivory solid 2" squares. Layer a marked square on a red text print square, right sides together. Sew ¼" from both sides of the drawn line. Cut the unit apart on the marked line. Make 36 half-square-triangle units and trim them to 1½" square, including seam allowances.

Make 36 units.

2 Lay out four triangle units from step 1 in two rows, rotating the units to form a pinwheel. Sew the units into rows and then join the rows to make a sashing unit. Make nine units measuring 2½" square, including seam allowances.

Make 9 units, 2½" × 2½".

3 Referring to the quilt assembly diagram on page 25, join three sashing units and two ivory solid 2½" × 18½" strips to make a sashing row. Make three rows measuring 2½" × 42½", including seam allowances.

4 Join three ivory solid 2½" × 18½" strips, one green block, and one red block to make a block row. Make two rows measuring 18½" × 42½", including seam allowances.

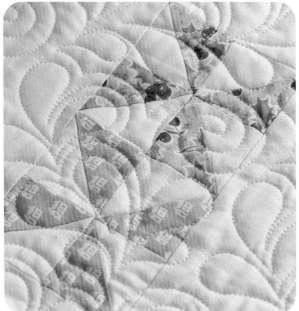

Charmed by Moda Bake Shop

5 Join the sashing rows and block rows, alternating their positions as shown. The quilt top should measure 42½" square, including seam allowances.

6 Join the ivory solid 1½"-wide strips end to end. From the pieced strip, cut two 44½"-long strips and two 42½"-long strips. Sew the shorter strips to the left and right sides of the quilt top. Sew the longer strips to the top and bottom edges. Press all seam allowances toward the border. The quilt top should measure 44½" square, including seam allowances.

7 Join the red pinecone print 3"-wide strips end to end. From the pieced strip, cut two 49½"-long strips and two 44½"-long strips. Sew the shorter strips to the left and right sides of the quilt top. Sew the longer strips to the top and bottom edges. Press all seam allowances toward the border. The quilt top should measure 49½" square.

Finishing the Quilt

For more details on any finishing steps, visit ShopMartingale.com/HowtoQuilt for free downloadable information.

1 Layer the quilt top with batting and backing; baste the layers together.

2 Quilt by hand or machine. Susan used the Citrine pantograph by Patricia Ritter to machine quilt an allover feather and swirl design.

3 Use the green 2½"-wide strips to make double-fold binding. Attach the binding to the quilt.

Quilt assembly

Flutter By

JEN DALY

Cute-as-a-button patchwork flowers, hearts, and butterflies make a fun "row" quilt, in which each row consists of a different garden-themed type of block. You won't be bored piecing this one! You may even want to take a cue from Jen and hand quilt your finished project.

FINISHED QUILT: 28" × 37"
FINISHED BLOCKS: 4" × 4", 5" × 4", and 5" × 9"

Materials

Yardage is based on 42"-wide fabric. A Moda Fabrics charm pack contains 42 squares, 5" × 5". Jen used Garden Gatherings by Primitive Gatherings for Moda Fabrics.

- ○ 1 charm pack *OR* 42 squares, 5" × 5", of assorted prints for blocks
- ○ 1 yard of cream print for blocks and sashing
- ○ ⅓ yard of green print for border
- ○ ⅓ yard of purple print for binding
- ○ 1¼ yards of fabric for backing
- ○ 34" × 43" piece of batting
- ○ Gold 6-strand embroidery floss for butterfly antennae

Cutting

All measurements include ¼" seam allowances. Before you begin cutting, see "Plan Ahead," above. Label your pieces as you cut. The assembly diagrams refer to each piece by the letter that follows the dimensions.

HEART BLOCKS

From *each of 5* assorted print squares, cut:
2 pieces, 2½" × 4½" (10 total; A)

BUTTERFLY BLOCKS

From *each of 4* assorted print squares, cut:
4 squares, 2½" × 2½" (16 total; B)

From *each of 2* assorted print squares, cut:
2 pieces, 1½" × 2½" (4 total; C)

2 squares, 1½" × 1½" (4 total; L. Set aside for Rolling Stone Flower blocks.)

SPINNING FLOWER BLOCKS

From *each of 5* assorted print squares, cut:
4 squares, 2½" × 2½" (20 total; D)

From *each of 3* assorted print squares, cut:
8 squares, 1½" × 1½" (24 total, 4 are extra; E)

CROSS FLOWER BLOCKS

From *each of 6* assorted print squares, cut:
1 square, 2½" × 2½" (6 total, 1 is extra; F)
4 pieces, 1½" × 2½" (24 total, 4 are extra; G)

DAISY BLOCKS

From *each of 5* assorted print squares, cut:
4 squares, 2½" × 2½" (20 total; H)

From *each of 2* assorted print squares, cut:
12 squares, 1¼" × 1¼" (24 total, 4 are extra; I)

ROLLING STONE FLOWER BLOCKS

From *each of 4* assorted print squares, cut:
4 squares, 2½" × 2½" (16 total; J)

From *each of 2* assorted print squares, cut:
8 squares, 1½" × 1½" (16 total; K)

From *each of 4* assorted print squares, cut:
2 squares, 2½" × 2½" (8 total; M)
1 strip, 1½" × 4½" (4 total; N)

ADDITIONAL CUTTING

From the cream print, cut:

2 strips, 2½" × 42"; crosscut into 18 squares, 2½" × 2½"

9 strips, 1½" × 42"; crosscut into:
- 3 strips, 1½" × 9½"
- 3 strips, 1½" × 4½"
- 196 squares, 1½" × 1½"

8 strips, 1¼" × 42"; crosscut into:
- 6 strips, 1¼" × 25"
- 2 strips, 1¼" × 9½"
- 26 strips, 1¼" × 4½"

1 strip, 1" × 42"; crosscut into 40 squares, 1" × 1"

From the green print, cut:

4 strips, 2" × 42"; crosscut into:
- 2 strips, 2" × 34"
- 2 strips, 2" × 28"

From the purple print, cut:

4 strips, 2½" × 42"

Making the Heart Blocks

Press seam allowances in the directions indicated by the arrows.

1 Draw a diagonal line from corner to corner on the wrong side of 20 cream 1½" squares and 10 cream 2½" squares.

2 Place a marked 1½" square on the upper-left corner of an A piece. Sew on the marked line. Trim the excess corner fabric ¼" from the stitched line. Place a marked 1½" square on the upper-right corner of the A piece. Sew and trim as before. Make 10 units measuring 2½" × 4½", including seam allowances.

Make 10 units,
2½" × 4½".

3 Join matching units from step 2 in pairs to make five units measuring 4½" square, including seam allowances.

Make 5 units,
4½" × 4½".

4 Place a marked 2½" square from step 1 on the lower-left corner of a unit from step 3. Sew on the marked line. Trim the excess corner fabric ¼" from the stitched line. Place a marked 2½" square on the lower-right corner of the unit. Sew and trim as before. Make five Heart blocks measuring 4½" square, including seam allowances.

Make 5 blocks,
4½" × 4½".

Making the Butterfly Blocks

1 Draw a diagonal line from corner to corner on the wrong side of 32 cream 1½" squares.

2 Place marked squares on opposite corners of a B square. Sew on the marked lines. Trim the excess corner fabric ¼" from the stitched lines. Make 16 wing units measuring 2½" square, including seam allowances.

Make 16 units,
2½" × 2½".

3 Join two cream 1½" squares and one C piece. Make four butterfly body units measuring 1½" × 4½", including seam allowances.

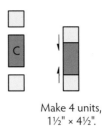

Make 4 units,
1½" × 4½".

4 Lay out four matching wing units and one butterfly body unit in columns, noting the direction of the pressed seam allowances. Sew the wing units into columns and then join the columns. Make four Butterfly blocks measuring 5½" × 4½", including seam allowances.

Make 4 blocks,
5½" × 4½".

Making the Spinning Flower Blocks

1 Draw a diagonal line from corner to corner on the wrong side of 20 E squares and 20 cream 1½" squares.

2 Place a marked E square on the lower-right corner of a D square. Sew on the marked line. Trim the excess corner fabric ¼" from the stitched line. Press the seam allowances toward D on 10 units and toward E on the remaining 10 units. Place a marked cream square on the lower-left corner of the D square. Sew and trim as before. Make 20 petal units measuring 2½" square, including seam allowances.

Make 10 of each unit,
2½" × 2½".

3 Lay out four matching petal units in two rows of two, noting the directions of the pressed seam allowances. Sew the units into rows and then join the rows. Make five Spinning Flower blocks measuring 4½" square, including seam allowances.

Make 5 blocks,
4½" × 4½".

Making the Cross Flower Blocks

Lay out four cream 1½" squares, four matching G pieces, and one contrasting F square in three rows as shown. Sew the pieces into rows and then join the rows. Make five Cross Flower blocks measuring 4½" square, including seam allowances.

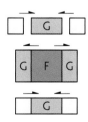

Make 5 blocks,
4½" × 4½".

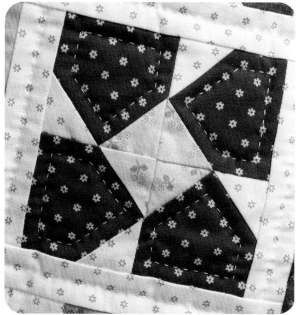

Designed, pieced, and hand quilted by Jen Daly.

See more of Jen's designs at JenDalyQuilts.com.

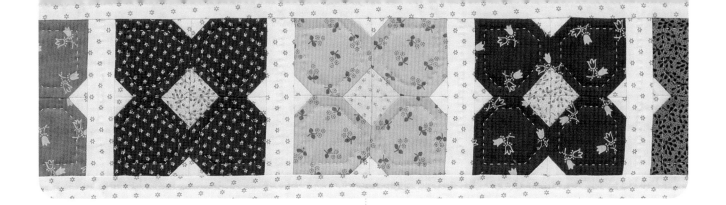

Making the Daisy Blocks

1 Draw a diagonal line from corner to corner on the wrong side of 20 I squares and 40 cream 1" squares.

2 Place a marked I square on the lower-right corner of an H square. Sew on the marked line. Trim the excess corner fabric ¼" from the stitched line. Place marked cream squares on the upper-right and lower-left corners of the H square. Sew and trim as before. Make 20 petal units measuring 2½" square, including seam allowances.

Make 20 units,
2½" × 2½".

3 Lay out four matching petal units in two rows of two. Sew the units into rows and then join the rows. Make five Daisy blocks measuring 4½" square, including seam allowances.

Make 5 blocks,
4½" × 4½".

Making the Rolling Stone Flower Blocks

1 Draw a diagonal line from corner to corner on the wrong side of 80 cream 1½" squares.

2 Place marked squares on opposite corners of a J square. Sew on the marked lines. Trim the excess corner fabric ¼" from the stitched lines. Place marked squares on the remaining corners of the J square. Sew and trim as before. Make 16 petal units measuring 2½" square, including seam allowances.

Make 16 units,
2½" × 2½".

3 Join a K square and a cream 1½" square to make a side unit. Make 16 side units measuring 1½" × 2½", including seam allowances.

Make 16 units,
1½" × 2½".

4 Lay out four matching petal units, four matching side units, and one L square in three rows, rotating the side units as shown. Sew the pieces into rows and then join the rows. Make four flower units measuring 5½" square, including seam allowances.

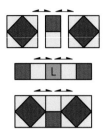

Make 4 units,
5½" × 5½".

5 Place marked squares from step 1 on opposite corners of an M square. Sew on the marked lines. Trim the excess corner fabric ¼" from the stitched lines. Make eight leaf units measuring 2½" square, including seam allowances.

Make 8 units,
2½" × 2½".

6 Lay out two cream 2½" squares, two matching leaf units, and one matching N strip in three columns as shown. Sew the pieces into columns and then join the columns. Make four stem/leaf units measuring 4½" × 5½", including seam allowances.

Make 4 units,
4½" × 5½".

7 Join one flower unit and one stem/leaf unit to make a block. Make four Rolling Stone Flower blocks measuring 5½" × 9½", including seam allowances.

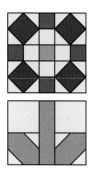
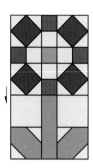

Make 4 blocks,
5½" × 9½".

Assembling the Quilt Top

Refer to the quilt assembly diagram on page 35 as needed throughout.

1 For row A, join six cream 1¼" × 4½" strips and the five Heart blocks to make a row that measures 4½" × 25", including seam allowances.

2 For row B, join two cream 1¼" × 4½" strips, three cream 1½" × 4½" strips, and the four Butterfly blocks to make a row that measures 4½" × 25", including seam allowances.

3 For row C, join six cream 1¼" × 4½" strips and the five Spinning Flower blocks to make a row that measures 4½" × 25", including seam allowances.

4 For row D, join six cream 1¼" × 4½" strips and the five Cross Flower blocks to make a row that measures 4½" × 25", including seam allowances.

5 For row E, join six cream 1¼" × 4½" strips and the five Daisy blocks to make a row that measures 4½" × 25", including seam allowances.

Charmed by Moda Bake Shop

6 For row F, join two cream 1¼" × 9½" strips, three cream 1½" × 9½" strips, and the four Rolling Stone Flower blocks to make a row that measures 9½" × 25", including seam allowances.

7 Join the six cream 1¼" × 25" strips and the block rows, alternating their positions as shown. The quilt top should measure 25" × 34", including seam allowances.

8 Sew the green 2" × 34" strips to the left and right sides of the quilt top. Sew the green 2" × 28" strips to the top and bottom edges. Press seam allowances toward the border. The quilt top should measure 28" × 37".

Finishing the Quilt

For more details on any finishing steps, visit ShopMartingale.com/HowtoQuilt for free downloadable information.

1 Layer the quilt top with batting and backing; baste the layers together.

2 Quilt by hand or machine. Jen hand quilted the quilt shown with echo stitching along the seamlines and straight lines in the sashing and border.

3 Use three strands of gold embroidery floss and a stem stitch to stitch two antennae on each butterfly as shown in the photo on page 29.

4 Use the purple 2½"-wide strips to make double-fold binding. Attach the binding to the quilt.

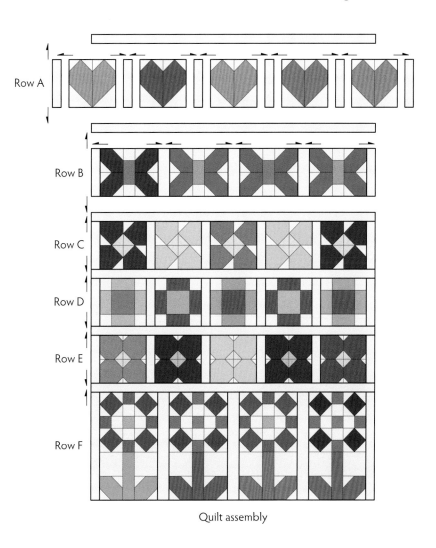

Quilt assembly

Flutter By

Sentimentally Yours

SHARLA KRENZEL

Something many quilters love is combining two easy-to-sew block designs to create a visually dynamic secondary design, as Sharla did here. Connect the dots in the chains to find your way to the little lavender and green hearts.

FINISHED QUILT: 60½" × 84½"
FINISHED BLOCK: 12" × 12"

Materials

Yardage is based on 42"-wide fabric. A Moda Fabrics charm pack contains 42 squares, 5"×5". Sharla used Wild Iris by Holly Taylor for Moda Fabrics.

○ 2 charm packs *OR* 63 squares, 5" × 5", of assorted purple and green prints for blocks

○ 3⅞ yards of eggshell solid for blocks

○ 1¾ yards of dark purple print for blocks and binding

○ 5¼ yards of fabric for backing

○ 69" × 93" piece of batting

Cutting

All measurements include ¼" seam allowances.

From *each of 27* assorted print squares, cut:
4 squares, 2½" × 2½" (108 total)

From *each of 36* assorted print squares, cut:
2 pieces, 2½" × 4½" (72 total)

From the eggshell solid, cut:
16 strips, 4½" × 42"; crosscut into 121 squares, 4½" × 4½"
21 strips, 2½" × 42"; crosscut *12 of the strips* into 180 squares, 2½" × 2½"

From the dark purple print, cut:
22 strips, 2½" × 42"; crosscut *5 of the strips* into 72 squares, 2½" × 2½"

Making the Heart Blocks

Press seam allowances in the directions indicated by the arrows.

1 Lay out one eggshell 2½" square, one eggshell 4½" square, and two different print 2½" × 4½" pieces in two rows as shown. Sew the pieces into rows and then join the rows. Make 36 units measuring 6½" square, including seam allowances.

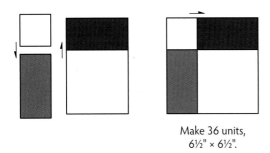

Make 36 units,
6½" × 6½".

2 Lay out four eggshell 2½" squares, two dark purple squares, and three assorted print squares from one color family in three rows as shown. Sew the squares into rows and then join the rows. Make 36 nine-patch units measuring 6½" square, including seam allowances.

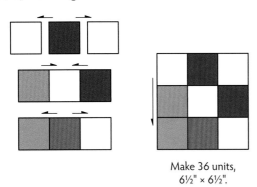

Make 36 units,
6½" × 6½".

3 Lay out two units from step 1 and two nine-patch units from step 2 in two rows as shown above right. Sew the units into rows and then join the rows to make a Heart block. Press the seam allowances in a counterclockwise direction (see

"Press for Success" on page 39). Make 18 blocks measuring 12½" square, including seam allowances.

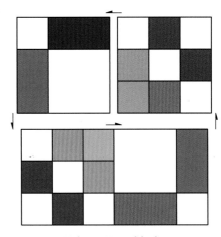

Make 18 Heart blocks,
12½" × 12½".

Making the Chain A and Chain B Blocks

1 Join one eggshell and one dark purple 2½" × 42" strip along their long edges. Make nine strip sets measuring 4½" × 42", including seam allowances. Cut the strip sets into 136 segments, 2½" × 4½".

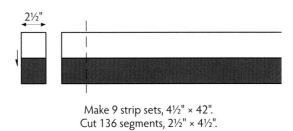

2½"

Make 9 strip sets, 4½" × 42".
Cut 136 segments, 2½" × 4½".

2 Join two segments to make a four-patch unit. Press the seam allowances in a counterclockwise direction (see "Press for Success"). Make 68 units measuring 4½" square, including seam allowances.

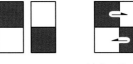

Make 68 units,
4½" × 4½".

Charmed by Moda Bake Shop

Press for Success

Spinning the center seam allowances reduces the bulk in the middle of the block by distributing the fabric evenly on all sides of the seam intersection. It also orients all the seam allowances in the same direction so that they will nest against opposing seam allowances in other blocks regardless of the orientation of the blocks. After you sew the seam, use a seam ripper to remove one or two stitches from the crossed seam. Then reposition the seam allowances to evenly distribute the fabric. If your seam allowances are pressed correctly, the center will look like a mini four patch.

3 Lay out five eggshell 4½" squares and four of the four-patch units in three rows, noting the orientation of the four-patch units. Sew the pieces into rows and then join the rows to make Chain block A. Make eight Chain A blocks measuring 12½" square, including seam allowances.

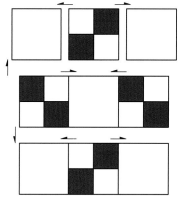

Make 8 Chain A blocks,
12½" × 12½".

4 Repeat step 3, noting the orientation of the four-patch units, to make nine Chain B blocks measuring 12½" square, including seam allowances.

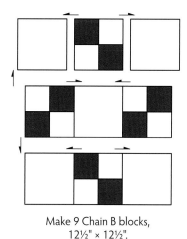

Make 9 Chain B blocks,
12½" × 12½".

Designed, pieced, and quilted by Sharla Krenzel.

Follow Sharla on Instagram @thistlethicketstudio.

Assembling the Quilt Top

Refer to the quilt assembly diagram below as needed throughout.

1 Join three Heart blocks and two Chain A blocks to make a row. Make four rows measuring 12½" × 60½", including seam allowances.

2 Join three Chain B blocks and two Heart blocks to make a row. Make three rows measuring 12½" × 60½", including seam allowances.

3 Join the rows, alternating their positions as shown. The quilt top should measure 60½" × 84½".

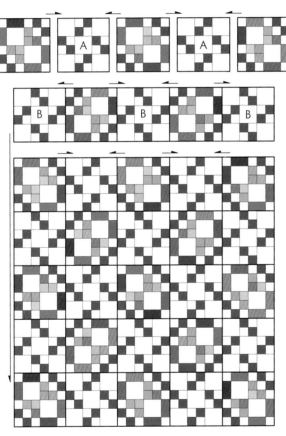

Quilt assembly

Finishing the Quilt

For more details on any finishing steps, visit ShopMartingale.com/HowtoQuilt for free downloadable information.

1 Since this quilt doesn't have a border, stitch around the perimeter of the quilt top, ⅛" from the outer edges, to lock the seams in place before quilting.

2 Layer the quilt top with batting and backing; baste the layers together.

3 Quilt by hand or machine. Sharla's quilt is machine quilted with an allover pattern of interlocking diagonal lines.

4 Use the remaining dark purple 2½"-wide strips to make double-fold binding. Attach the binding to the quilt.

Charming Pots

NICOLA DODD

One charm pack and beginner-friendly techniques are all it takes to cheer up your table with some everlasting blooms. Alternating the direction of every other pot means every seat at the table has a pretty posey in view!

FINISHED QUILT: 23" × 56"
FINISHED BLOCK: 4½" × 13½"

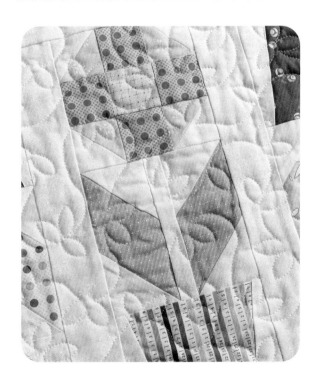

Materials

Yardage is based on 42"-wide fabric. A Moda Fabrics charm pack contains 42 squares, 5" × 5". Nicola used Beautiful Day by Corey Yoder for Moda Fabrics.

- 1 charm pack *OR* 32 squares, 5" × 5", of assorted prints for blocks
- 1 yard of white solid for blocks, sashing, and inner border
- ½ yard of pink diagonal check for outer border
- ½ yard of green print for binding
- 1¾ yards of fabric for backing
- 29" × 62" piece of batting

Plan Ahead

Before cutting the 5" squares, plan the fabric placement. Referring to the photo on page 46 for guidance, choose eight squares for the pots and label them as fabric A. Select eight squares for the leaves and label them as fabric B. Select eight squares for the sides of the flower units and label them as fabric C. Select four squares for the corners of the flower units and label them as fabric D. Choose four squares for the flower centers and label them as fabric E.

Cutting

All measurements include ¼" seam allowances. Before cutting, see "Plan Ahead," above, to group and label the squares A–E. As you cut, keep pieces grouped by letter.

From *each* of the B squares, cut:
2 pieces, 2½" × 5" (16 total)

From *each* of the C squares, cut:
4 squares, 2" × 2" (32 total)

From the E squares, cut a *total* of:
8 squares, 2" × 2"

From the white solid, cut:
1 strip, 5" × 42"; crosscut into:
- 4 squares, 5" × 5"
- 8 strips, 1" × 5"

2 strips, 2½" × 42"; crosscut into 32 squares, 2½" × 2½"
10 strips, 2" × 42"; crosscut *7 of the strips* into:
- 9 strips, 2" × 14"
- 16 strips, 2" × 5½"

From the pink diagonal check, cut:
4 strips, 3½" × 42"; crosscut *1 of the strips* into 2 strips, 3½" × 17"

From the green print, cut:
5 strips, 2½" × 42"

Making the Blocks

Press seam allowances in the directions indicated by the arrows.

1 Place two white 2" × 5½" strips right sides together. Place a ruler 1" in from the upper-left corner and angle it to meet the lower-right corner as shown. Cut along the ruler's edge to make two mirror-image pieces. Repeat to make eight pairs of mirror-image pieces.

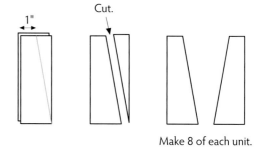

Make 8 of each unit.

2 Place a ruler on the right side of an A square ¼" down from the upper-left corner and angle it 1¼" in from the lower-left corner as shown. Mark a line along the edge of the ruler. In the same way, mark the other side of the square. Repeat to mark eight fabric A squares. *Do not cut on the marked lines.*

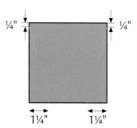

3 Place a trimmed piece from step 1 on top of a marked square, right sides together and aligning the angled edge of the white piece with the marked line. Sew ¼" from the edge of the trimmed piece. Repeat to sew a mirror-image piece to the opposite side of the square. Press. Flip the square to the wrong side and trim the white pieces even

Charmed by Moda Bake Shop

with the square. Then trim the excess corner fabric from the A squares ¼" from the stitched line. Make eight pot units measuring 5" square, including seam allowances.

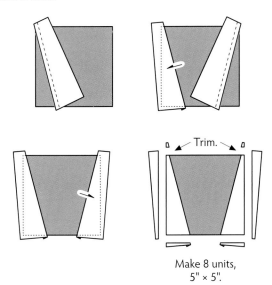

Make 8 units,
5" × 5".

4 Draw a diagonal line from corner to corner on the wrong side of the white 2½" squares. Place a marked square on one end of a B piece, right sides together. Sew on the marked line. Trim the excess corner fabric ¼" from the stitched line. Place a marked square on the opposite end of the B piece, noting the direction of the marked line. Sew and trim as before. Repeat to make a mirror-image unit, making sure to reverse the placement of the marked lines. Make eight pairs of leaf units measuring 2½" × 5", including seam allowances.

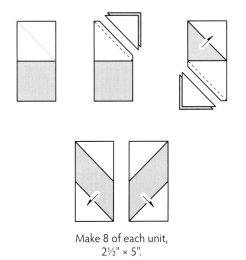

Make 8 of each unit,
2½" × 5".

5 Sew a leaf unit and matching mirror-image leaf unit to opposite sides of a white 1" × 5" strip. Make eight stem/leaf units measuring 5" square, including seam allowances.

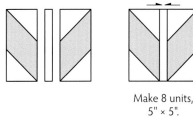

Make 8 units,
5" × 5".

6 Draw a diagonal line from corner to corner in both directions to form an X on the wrong side of the white 5" squares. Layer a marked square on top of a D square, right sides together. Sew ¼" from both sides of the drawn lines. Cut the units apart horizontally and vertically first. Then cut the units apart on the drawn lines to yield eight half-square-triangle units. Make 32 units and trim them to 2" square, including seam allowances.

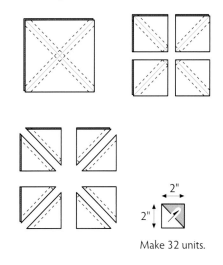

Make 32 units.

Designed and pieced by Nicola Dodd; quilted by Jayne Brereton.

See more of Nicola's work at CakeStandQuilts.com.

7 Lay out four matching half-square-triangle units, four matching fabric C squares, and one contrasting fabric E square in three rows, rotating the triangle units as shown. Sew the pieces into rows and then join the rows. Make eight flower units measuring 5" square, including seam allowances.

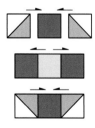

Make 8 units,
5" × 5".

8 Join one flower unit, one stem/leaf unit, and one pot unit to make a block. Make eight blocks measuring 5" × 14", including seam allowances.

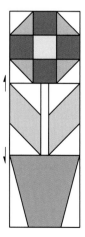

Make 8 blocks,
5" × 14".

Charmed by Moda Bake Shop

Assembling the Table Runner

1 Referring to the table-runner assembly diagram below, join the blocks and the white 2" × 14" strips, alternating their positions as shown. The table runner should measure 14" × 50", including seam allowances.

2 Join the remaining white 2"-wide strips end to end. From the pieced strip, cut two 50"-long strips. Sew the strips to the long sides of the runner. The table runner should measure 17" × 50", including seam allowances.

3 Sew the pink 3½" × 17" strips to the short ends of the table runner. Join the remaining pink 3½"-wide strips end to end. From the pieced strip, cut two 56"-long strips. Sew the strips to the long sides of the runner. The table runner should measure 23" × 56".

Finishing the Table Runner

For more details on any finishing steps, visit ShopMartingale.com/HowtoQuilt for free downloadable information.

1 Layer the table-runner top with batting and backing; baste the layers together.

2 Quilt by hand or machine. Nicola's table runner is machine quilted with an allover design of curved lines and leaves.

3 Use the green 2½"-wide strips to make double-fold binding. Attach the binding to the table runner.

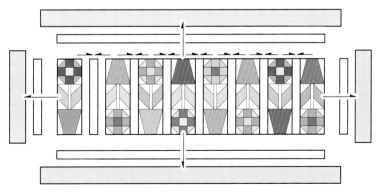

Table-runner assembly

Charming Stars

LISSA ALEXANDER

Attention all star lovers! Choosing a charm pack with an equal number of lights and darks as Lissa did will enable you to have the dark stars pop and the light ones subtly shimmer in the background. Of course, a scrappier charm pack of lights, mediums, and darks would give you a more varied effect. The choice is yours!

FINISHED QUILT: 59" × 68"
FINISHED BLOCK: 4½" × 4½"

Materials

Yardage is based on 42"-wide fabric. A Moda Fabrics charm pack contains 42 squares, 5" × 5". Lissa used Newport by Minick & Simpson for Moda Fabrics.

- 2 charm packs OR:
  - 42 squares, 5" × 5", of assorted dark prints for patchwork
  - 30 squares, 5" × 5", of assorted light prints for patchwork
- 2½ yards of ivory solid for blocks and border
- 1⅛ yards of gray solid for blocks
- ⅝ yard of navy diagonal stripe for binding
- 3⅝ yards of fabric for backing
- 65" × 74" piece of batting

Cutting

All measurements include ¼" seam allowances.

From the ivory solid, cut:
16 strips, 5" × 42"; crosscut into 123 squares, 5" × 5"

From the gray solid, cut:
17 strips, 2" × 42"; crosscut into 336 squares, 2" × 2"

From the navy diagonal stripe, cut:
7 strips, 2½" × 42"

Making the Blocks

Press seam allowances in the directions indicated by the arrows.

1 Draw a diagonal line from corner to corner on the wrong side of the gray squares. Place marked squares on the corners of an ivory 5" square. Sew on the marked lines. Trim the excess corner fabric ¼" from the stitched lines. Make 71 Snowball blocks measuring 5" square, including seam allowances.

 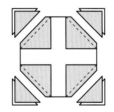

Make 71 blocks,
5" × 5".

2 Place marked squares from step 1 on adjacent corners of an ivory 5" square. Sew on the marked lines. Trim the excess corner fabric ¼" from the stitched lines. Make 26 border blocks measuring 5" square, including seam allowances.

 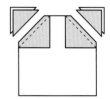

Make 26 blocks,
5" × 5".

Assembling the Quilt Top

1 Join six dark 5" squares and five Snowball blocks to make a row. Make seven A rows measuring 5" × 50", including seam allowances.

Make 7 A block rows,
5" × 50".

2 Join six Snowball blocks and five light 5" squares to make a row. Make six B rows measuring 5" × 50", including seam allowances.

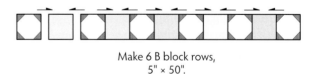

Make 6 B block rows,
5" × 50".

3 Referring to the quilt assembly diagram on page 52, join the A and B rows, alternating their positions as shown. The quilt top should measure 50" × 59", including seam allowances.

Charmed by Moda Bake Shop

Designed by Lissa Alexander; quilted by Maggi Honeyman.

Follow Lissa's quilting adventures on her blog,
ModaLissa.com, or @ModaLissa on Instagram.

5 Sew the side borders to the left and right sides of the quilt top. Add the top and bottom borders. The quilt top should measure 59" × 68".

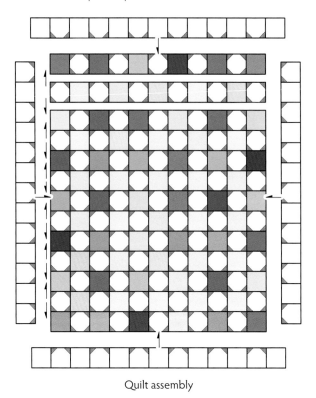

Quilt assembly

4 Join seven border blocks and six ivory squares to make a side border measuring 5" × 59", including seam allowances. Make two. Join seven ivory squares and six border blocks to make a top border measuring 5" × 59", including seam allowances. Repeat to make a bottom border.

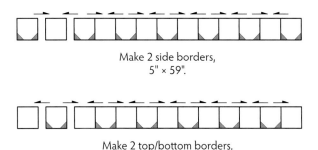

Make 2 side borders,
5" × 59".

Make 2 top/bottom borders,
5" × 59".

Finishing the Quilt

For more details on any finishing steps, visit ShopMartingale.com/HowtoQuilt for free downloadable information.

1 Since this quilt doesn't have a border of long strips, stitch around the perimeter of the quilt top, 1/8" from the outer edges, to lock the seams in place.

2 Layer the quilt top with batting and backing; baste the layers together.

3 Quilt by hand or machine. Lissa's quilt is machine quilted with a feathered wreath in the Snowball and Border blocks. A star motif is stitched in the light, dark, and border squares.

4 Use the navy 2½"-wide strips to make double-fold binding. Attach the binding to the quilt.

Charmed by Moda Bake Shop

Strolling Pathway

MICHELE KUHNS

Don't be afraid to stray off the beaten path. That's what Michele did with her design, which makes an unexpected turn in the middle. Taking a different route can lead to adventures and sights you might otherwise miss.

FINISHED QUILT: 72½" × 72½"
FINISHED BLOCK: 16" × 16"

Materials

Yardage is based on 42"-wide fabric. A Moda Fabrics charm pack contains 42 squares, 5"×5". Michele used Slow Stroll by Fancy That Design House & Co. for Moda Fabrics.

- 3 charm packs OR 108 squares, 5" × 5", of assorted prints for blocks and setting
- 4 yards of eggshell solid for blocks and setting
- ⅝ yard of green print for binding
- 4½ yards of fabric for backing
- 79" × 79" piece of batting

Plan Ahead

Plan your fabric combinations before cutting the 5" squares. For each of the 16 blocks, choose four 5" squares from the same color family. Label two squares as fabric A and two squares as fabric B. Then select two 5" squares from a contrasting print and label them as fabric C. Repeat to make 16 sets of fabric A–C squares. Label the remaining 12 squares as fabric D. Keep in mind that prints from the same color family as the eggshell background will blend in and be lost in the overall design. For best results, choose prints that stand out against the background.

Cutting

All measurements include ¼" seam allowances. Before cutting, see "Plan Ahead," above, to label the A–C squares.

From *each* of the B squares, cut:
1 square, 4½" × 4½" (32 total)

From *each* of the C squares, cut:
1 square, 4½" × 4½" (32 total)

From *each* of the D squares, cut:
1 square, 4½" × 4½" (12 total)

From the eggshell solid, cut:
3 strips, 8½" × 42"; crosscut into:
  - 3 strips, 8½" × 20½"
  - 1 square, 8½" × 8½"
4 strips, 5" × 42"; crosscut into 32 squares, 5" × 5"
19 strips, 4½" × 42"; crosscut into:
  - 37 pieces, 4½" × 8½"
  - 76 squares, 4½" × 4½"

From the green print, cut:
8 strips, 2½" × 42"

Making the Blocks

Press seam allowances in the directions indicated by the arrows.

1 Draw a diagonal line from corner to corner on the wrong side of the eggshell 5" squares. Layer a marked square on a fabric A square, right sides together. Sew ¼" from both sides of the drawn line. Cut the unit apart on the marked line. Make two half-square-triangle units and trim them to 4½" square, including seam allowances. Repeat to make 16 sets of four matching half-square-triangle units.

Make 16 sets of
4 matching units.

2 Lay out four eggshell 4½" squares, two eggshell 4½" × 8½" pieces, four matching half-square-triangle units, two fabric B squares from the same color family, and two contrasting fabric C squares in four rows, noting the orientation of the triangle units. Sew all the pieces into rows and then join the rows. Make 16 blocks measuring 16½" square, including seam allowances.

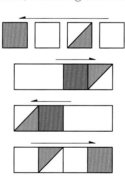 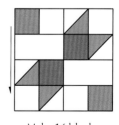

Make 16 blocks,
16½" × 16½".

Making the Sashing Rows

1 Lay out two eggshell 4½" squares and two assorted fabric D squares in two rows of two squares each. Sew the squares into rows and then join the rows. Make six four-patch units measuring 8½" square, including seam allowances.

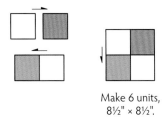

Make 6 units,
8½" × 8½".

2 Join two eggshell 4½" × 8½" pieces, two four-patch units, and one eggshell 8½" square to make the top sashing row. The row should measure 8½" × 32½", including seam allowances.

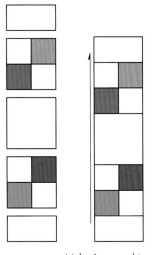

Make 1 top sashing row,
8½" × 32½".

3 Join one eggshell 4½" × 8½" piece, one four-patch unit, and one eggshell 8½" × 20½" strip to make the bottom sashing row. The row should measure 8½" × 32½", including seam allowances.

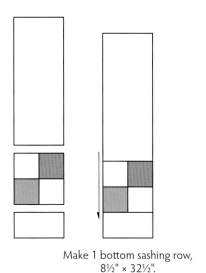

Make 1 bottom sashing row,
8½" × 32½".

4 Join together two eggshell 4½" × 8½" pieces, three four-patch units, and two eggshell 8½" × 20½" strips to make the center sashing row, noting the orientation of the center unit. The row should measure 8½" × 72½", including seam allowances.

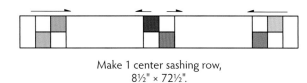

Make 1 center sashing row,
8½" × 72½".

Charmed by Moda Bake Shop

Designed, pieced, and quilted by Michele Kuhns.

See more of Michele's patterns on Instagram @crayonboxquiltstudio.

Assembling the Quilt Top

1 Lay out four blocks in two rows of two as shown. Sew the blocks into rows and then join the rows. Make four quadrants measuring 32½" square, including seam allowances.

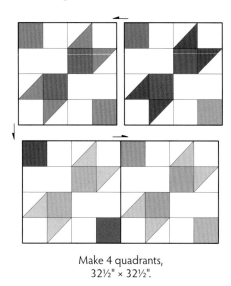

Make 4 quadrants,
32½" × 32½".

2 Referring to the quilt assembly diagram below, lay out the four quadrants and the sashing rows, alternating their positions as shown. Join the quadrants and sashing rows to make the top and bottom rows. Then join the top and bottom rows to the center sashing row. The quilt top should measure 72½" square.

Finishing the Quilt

For more details on any finishing steps, visit ShopMartingale.com/HowtoQuilt for free downloadable information.

1 Since this quilt doesn't have a border, stitch around the perimeter of the quilt top, ⅛" from the outer edges, to lock the seams in place before quilting.

2 Layer the quilt top with batting and backing; baste the layers together.

3 Quilt by hand or machine. Michele's quilt is machine quilted with an allover swirl design.

4 Use the green 2½"-wide strips to make double-fold binding. Attach the binding to the quilt.

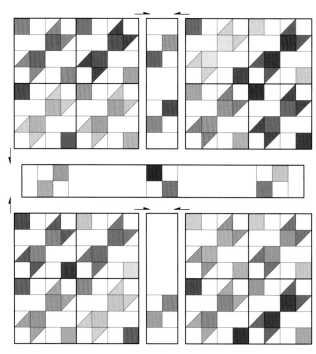

Quilt assembly

Charmed by Moda Bake Shop

Radiate

CHRISTINE WELD

Make delightful use of all the beautiful colors found in a charm pack when you combine both high- and low-contrast units. Using a clever quadrant technique, constructing a striking layout is easy!

FINISHED QUILT: 54½" × 62½"

Materials

Yardage is based on 42"-wide fabric. A Moda Fabrics charm pack contains 42 squares, 5"×5". Christine used Nantucket Summer by Camille Roskelley for Moda Fabrics.

○ 2 charm packs *OR* 36 pairs of matching squares, 5" × 5", of assorted prints for blocks

○ 1⅞ yards of white solid for blocks and setting

○ ¾ yard of navy print for border

○ ⅝ yard of blue stripe for binding

○ 3½ yards of fabric for backing

○ 61" × 69" piece of batting

Cutting

All measurements include ¼" seam allowances.

From the white solid, cut:
9 strips, 5" × 42"; crosscut into 72 squares, 5" × 5"
3 strips, 4½" × 42"; crosscut into 24 squares,
    4½" × 4½"

From the navy print, cut:
6 strips, 3½" × 42"

From the blue stripe, cut:
7 strips, 2½" × 42"

Making the Half-Square-Triangle Units

Press seam allowances in the directions indicated by the arrows.

Draw a diagonal line from corner to corner on the wrong side of the white 5" squares. Layer a marked square on a print square, right sides together. Sew ¼" from both sides of the drawn line. Cut the unit apart on the marked line. Make two half-square-triangle units and trim them to 4½" square, including seam allowances. Repeat to make 36 sets of four matching units.

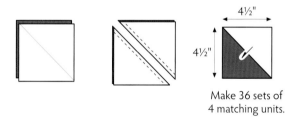

Make 36 sets of
4 matching units.

Assembling the Quilt Top

The quilt is constructed in quadrants. Refer to the photo on page 62 as needed throughout.

1 Divide the half-square-triangle units into four identical stacks of 36 units each.

2 Lay out one stack of 36 units and six white squares in seven rows, noting the color placement along the bottom and side edges. Sew the pieces into rows and then join the rows. Make two identical quadrants measuring 24½" × 28½", including seam allowances.

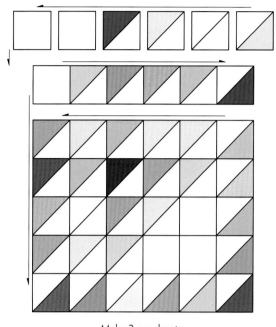

Make 2 quadrants,
24½" × 28½".

3 Repeat step 2 to make two mirror-image quadrants measuring 24½" × 28½", including seam allowances.

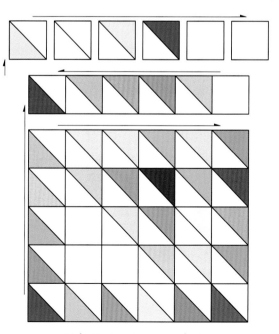

Make 2 mirror-image quadrants,
24½" × 28½".

Designed, pieced, and quilted by Christine Weld.

Follow Christine on Instagram @christine.weld.

4 Lay out the four quadrants, placing identical quadrants diagonally opposite each other and rotating the quadrants so that matching units form a diamond shape in the center. Matching units should form flying-geese units that point toward the outer edges. Sew the quadrants into rows and then join the rows. The quilt top should measure 48½" × 56½", including seam allowances.

5 Join the navy 3½"-wide strips end to end. From the pieced strip, cut two 56½"-long strips and two 54½"-long strips. Sew the longer strips to the left and right sides of the quilt top. Sew the shorter strips to the top and bottom edges. Press all seam allowances toward the borders. The quilt top should measure 54½" × 62½".

Finishing the Quilt

For more details on any finishing steps, visit ShopMartingale.com/HowtoQuilt for free downloadable information.

1 Layer the quilt top with batting and backing; baste the layers together.

2 Quilt by hand or machine. Christine's quilt is machine quilted with horizontal and vertical straight lines.

3 Use the blue stripe 2½"-wide strips to make double-fold binding. Attach the binding to the quilt.

Quilt assembly

All Boxed In

TAMMY VONDERSCHMITT

Tammy's clever use of color placement makes this petite quilt look both interesting and challenging. But, upon close inspection, she simply made Shoo Fly blocks with extra-plump centers in two different colorways. The secondary designs emerge where the blocks abut one another.

FINISHED QUILT: 26" × 26"
FINISHED BLOCK: 6" × 6"

Materials

Yardage is based on 42"-wide fabric. A Moda Fabrics charm pack contains 42 squares, 5" × 5". Tammy used Late October by Sweetwater for Moda Fabrics.

- 1 charm pack *OR:*
  - 9 squares, 5" × 5", of assorted orange prints for block A
  - 4 squares, 5" × 5", of assorted light prints for block B
  - 8 squares, 5" × 5", of assorted gray and black prints for blocks and setting triangles
- ⅝ yard of white solid for blocks and setting triangles
- ⅜ yard of navy solid for blocks and setting triangles
- ⅓ yard of orange diagonal check for binding
- 1 yard of fabric for backing
- 30" × 30" piece of batting

Cutting

All measurements include ¼" seam allowances.

From *each* of the assorted orange prints, cut:
1 square, 3½" × 3½" (9 total)

From *each* of the assorted light prints, cut:
1 square, 3½" × 3½" (4 total)

From *each* of the assorted gray and black prints, cut:
4 squares, 2½" × 2½" (32 total)

From the white solid, cut:
1 strip, 6" × 42"; crosscut into:
- 2 squares, 6" × 6"; cut into quarters diagonally to yield 8 side triangles
- 2 squares, 3½" × 3½"; cut in half diagonally to yield 4 corner triangles

2 strips, 2½" × 42"; crosscut into 32 squares, 2½" × 2½"

4 strips, 2" × 42"; crosscut into 36 pieces, 2" × 3½"

From the navy solid, cut:
5 strips, 2" × 42"; crosscut into:
- 4 strips, 2" × 7½"
- 16 strips, 2" × 6½"
- 16 pieces, 2" × 3½"

From the orange diagonal check, cut:
3 strips, 2½" × 42"

Making the Blocks

Press seam allowances in the directions indicated by the arrows.

1 Draw a diagonal line from corner to corner on the wrong side of the white 2½" squares. Layer a marked square on a gray or black square, right sides together. Sew ¼" from both sides of the drawn line. Cut the unit apart on the marked line.

Make 64 half-square-triangle units and trim them to 2" square, including seam allowances.

Make 64 units.

2 Lay out four matching half-square-triangle units, four white 2" × 3½" pieces, and one orange square in three rows, rotating the triangle units as shown. Sew the units into rows and then join the rows. Make nine A blocks measuring 6½" square, including seam allowances.

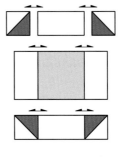 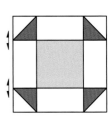

Make 9 A blocks, 6½" × 6½".

3 Lay out four matching half-square-triangle units, four navy 2" × 3½" pieces, and one light square in three rows, rotating the triangle units as shown. Sew the units into rows and then join the rows. Make four B blocks measuring 6½" square, including seam allowances.

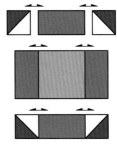 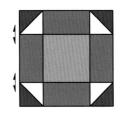

Make 4 B blocks, 6½" × 6½".

Charmed by Moda Bake Shop

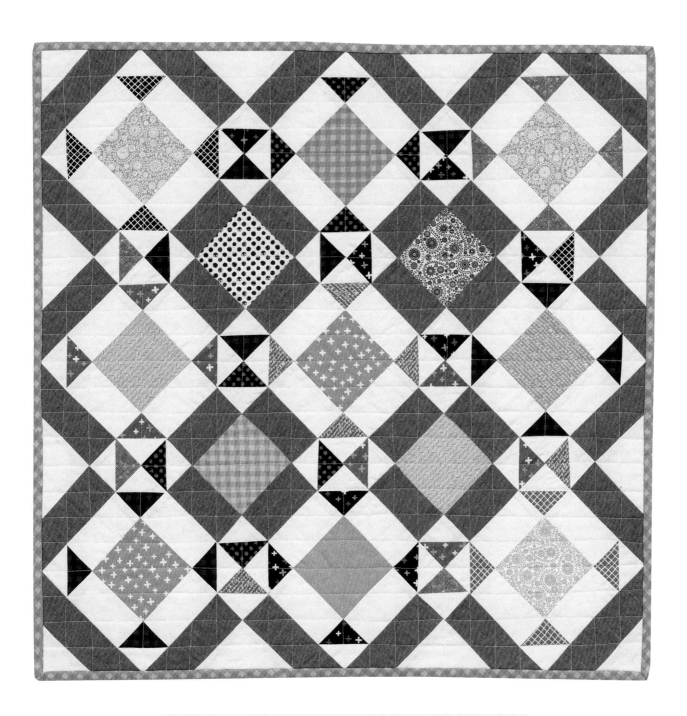

Designed, pieced, and quilted by Tammy Vonderschmitt.

See more of what Tammy is quilting on Instagram @nithaystack.

Radiate Joy

Tammy's quilt features orange centers in nine blocks and gray centers in four. If you want to achieve a look that radiates outward from the center, introduce a third color instead of orange for the center Churn dash block.

Assembling the Quilt Top

1 Join one half-square-triangle unit, two navy 2" × 6½" strips, and one white side triangle as shown. Make eight side units. You'll have four half-square-triangle units left over for another project.

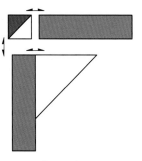

Make 8 side units.

2 Fold each white corner triangle in half and lightly crease to mark the center on the long side. Fold each navy 2" × 7½" strip in half and lightly crease to mark the center on the long side. Sew a white triangle to a navy strip, matching the center creases. Make four corner units.

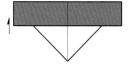

Make 4 corner units.

3 Referring to the quilt assembly diagram below, arrange and sew the A and B blocks together in diagonal rows, adding the side units to the ends of each row as indicated. Join the rows, adding the corner units last.

4 Trim and square up the quilt top, making sure to leave ¼" beyond the points of all the blocks for seam allowances. The quilt top should measure 26" square.

Finishing the Quilt

For more details on any finishing steps, visit ShopMartingale.com/HowtoQuilt for free downloadable information.

1 Since this quilt doesn't have a border, stitch around the perimeter of the quilt top, ⅛" from the outer edges, to lock the seams in place before quilting.

2 Layer the quilt top with batting and backing; baste the layers together.

3 Quilt by hand or machine. Tammy's quilt is machine quilted with straight lines to form a 1" crosshatched grid.

4 Use the orange check 2½"-wide strips to make double-fold bias binding. Attach the binding to the quilt.

Trim ¼" from point.

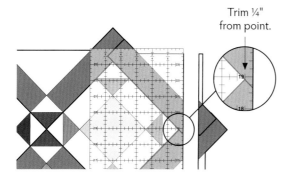

Quilt assembly

Pretty Posies

MELISSA CORRY

Grays, coral pinks, and a pop of gold combine for a chic, nearly-neutral color palette that's right on trend! Patchwork flowers dance across this quilt top, each offset a bit from the adjacent row, making it feel as if these blooms are blowing in a gentle breeze.

FINISHED QUILT: 54½" × 66½"
FINISHED BLOCK: 9" × 9"

Materials

Yardage is based on 42"-wide fabric. A Moda Fabrics charm pack contains 42 squares, 5" × 5". Melissa used Midnight in the Garden by Sweetfire Road for Moda Fabrics.

- 4 matching charm packs OR 150 squares, 5" × 5", of assorted prints for blocks*
- 3⅝ yards of gray solid for blocks, sashing, and border
- ⅝ yard of charcoal print for binding
- 3½ yards of fabric for backing
- 61" × 73" piece of batting

*You'll need 30 sets of 4 matching squares, plus an additional 30 squares.

Cutting

All measurements include ¼" seam allowances.

From *each of the 30* assorted print squares that aren't part of matching sets, cut:
4 squares, 2" × 2" (120 total)

From the gray solid, cut:
2 strips, 9½" × 42"; crosscut into 30 strips, 2" × 9½"
26 strips, 2¾" × 42"; crosscut into 360 squares, 2¾" × 2¾"
13 strips, 2" × 42"

From the charcoal print, cut:
7 strips, 2½" × 42"

Making the Blocks

Instructions are for making one block. Repeat to make a total of 30 blocks. Press seam allowances in the directions indicated by the arrows.

1 Draw a diagonal line from corner to corner on the wrong side of 12 gray squares and four matching print 2" squares.

2 Place marked gray squares on opposite corners of a print 5" square. Sew on the marked lines. Trim the excess corner fabric ¼" from the stitched lines. Make four matching units measuring 5" square, including seam allowances.

Make 4 units,
5" × 5".

3 Position a unit so that the pressed seam allowances point toward the upper-right corner and place a marked gray square on the upper-left corner of the unit. Place a contrasting marked print 2" square on top of the gray triangle in the lower-left corner. Sew on the marked lines. Trim the excess corner fabric ¼" from the stitched lines. Make two petal units measuring 5" square, including seam allowances.

Make 2 units,
5" × 5".

4 Position a unit from step 2 so that the pressed seam allowances point toward the lower-left corner, and place a marked gray square on the upper-left corner of the unit. Place a matching marked print 2" square on top of the gray triangle in the lower-left corner. Sew on the marked lines and then trim the excess corner fabric ¼" from the stitched lines. Make two petal units measuring 5" square, including seam allowances.

Make 2 units,
5" × 5".

5 Lay out the petal units in two rows of two units each, noting the direction of the pressed seam allowances so that the seam allowances will abut smoothly when you join the units. Sew the units into rows and then join the rows. Repeat to make a total of 30 blocks measuring 9½" square, including seam allowances.

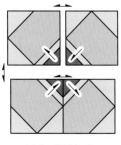

Make 30 blocks,
9½" × 9½".

Charmed by Moda Bake Shop

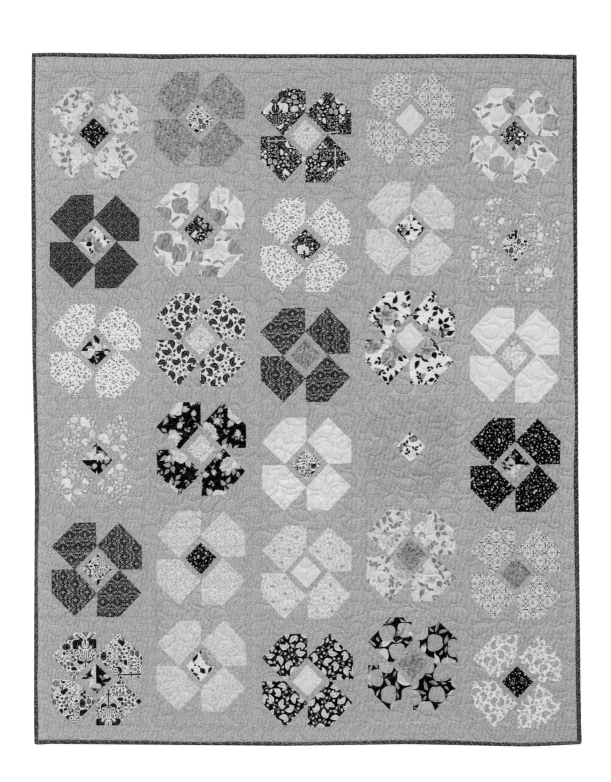

Designed, pieced, and quilted by Melissa Corry.

Find more of Melissa's patterns at HappyQuiltingMelissa.com.

Assembling the Quilt Top

1 Referring to the quilt assembly diagram below, join six blocks and six gray 2" × 9½" strips to make a column. Make five columns measuring 9½" × 63½", including seam allowances.

2 Join the gray 2"-wide strips end to end. From the pieced strip, cut six 63½"-long strips and two 54½"-long strips.

3 Join the block columns and four of the gray 63½"-long strips, alternating their positions as shown. The quilt top should measure 51½" × 63½", including seam allowances.

4 Sew the remaining gray 63½"-long strips to the left and right sides of the quilt top. Sew the

gray 54½"-long strips to the top and bottom edges. The quilt top should measure 54½" × 66½".

Finishing the Quilt

For more details on any finishing steps, visit ShopMartingale.com/HowtoQuilt for free downloadable information.

1 Layer the quilt top with batting and backing; baste the layers together.

2 Quilt by hand or machine. Melissa's quilt is machine quilted with an allover feather design.

3 Use the charcoal 2½"-wide strips to make double-fold binding. Attach the binding to the quilt.

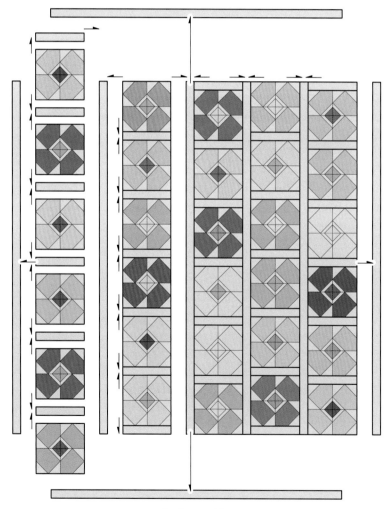

Quilt assembly

Charmed by Moda Bake Shop

Shoo Fly Spinners

JESSICA DAYON

Traditional Shoo Fly quilt blocks have center squares that are the same size as the triangles in the corners. In Jessica's blocks, she has slimmed down the center squares and added a fun border of mini squares, which means you can use almost every square inch of your charm square fabrics in this pretty quilt.

FINISHED QUILT: 56½" × 70½"
FINISHED BLOCK: 10" × 10"

Materials

Yardage is based on 42"-wide fabric. A Moda Fabrics charm pack contains 42 squares, 5" × 5". Jessica used Adamstown by Jo Morton for Moda Fabrics.

○ 1 charm pack *OR* 39 squares, 5" × 5", of assorted prints for blocks and border 3

○ 2⅝ yards of cream solid for blocks, sashing, and borders 2, 3, and 4

○ 1 yard of gold solid for sashing and border 1

○ ¾ yard of green print for border 5

○ ⅝ yard of brown print for binding

○ 3½ yards of fabric for backing

○ 63" × 77" piece of batting

Cutting

All measurements include ¼" seam allowances.

From *each of 3* assorted print squares, cut:
4 squares, 2½" × 2½" (12 total)

From *each of 12* assorted print squares, cut:
9 squares, 1½" × 1½" (108 total, 2 are extra)

From the cream solid, cut:
3 strips, 5" × 42"; crosscut into 24 squares, 5" × 5"
4 strips, 4½" × 42"; crosscut into:
    • 6 squares, 4½" × 4½"
    • 48 pieces, 2½" × 4½"
6 strips, 3" × 42"
6 strips, 2½" × 42"; crosscut into 17 strips,
    2½" × 10½"
6 strips, 2" × 42"
5 strips, 1½" × 42"; crosscut into 106 squares,
    1½" × 1½"

From the gold solid, cut:
2 strips, 2½" × 42"; crosscut into 24 squares,
    2½" × 2½"
17 strips, 1½" × 42"; crosscut *14 of the strips* into:
    • 2 strips, 1½" × 40½"
    • 34 strips, 1½" × 10½"

From the green print, cut:
7 strips, 3½" × 42"

From the brown print, cut:
7 strips, 2½" × 42"

Making the Blocks

Press seam allowances in the directions indicated by the arrows.

1 Draw a diagonal line from corner to corner on the wrong side of the cream 5" squares. Layer a marked square on a print 5" square, right sides together. Sew ¼" from both sides of the drawn line. Cut the unit apart on the marked line. Make 48

half-square-triangle units and trim them to 4½" square, including seam allowances.

Make 48 units.

2 Lay out four half-square-triangle units, four cream 2½" × 4½" pieces, and one print 2½" square in three rows, rotating the units as shown. Sew the pieces into rows and then join the rows. Make 12 blocks measuring 10½" square, including seam allowances.

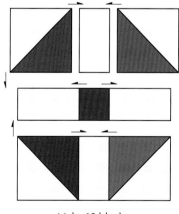

Make 12 blocks,
10½" × 10½".

Making the Sashing Units

1 Draw a diagonal line from corner to corner on the wrong side of the gold 2½" squares. Place marked squares on opposite corners of a cream 4½" square. Sew on the marked lines. Trim the excess corner fabric ¼" from the stitched lines. Place marked squares on the remaining corners of the square. Sew and trim as before. Make six square-in-a-square units measuring 4½" square, including seam allowances.

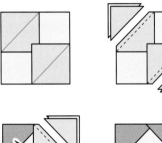

Make 6 units,
4½" × 4½".

2 Sew gold 1½" × 10½" strips to the long sides of a cream 2½" × 10½" strip to make a strip set. Make 17 strip sets measuring 4½" × 10½", including seam allowances.

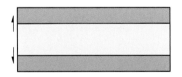

Make 17 strip units,
4½" × 10½".

Assembling the Quilt Top

1 Join three blocks and two strip sets to make a block row. Make four rows measuring 10½" × 38½", including seam allowances.

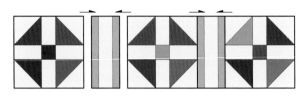

Make 4 block rows,
10½" × 38½".

2 Join three strip sets and two square-in-a-square units to make a sashing row. Make three rows measuring 4½" × 38½", including seam allowances.

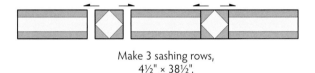

Make 3 sashing rows,
4½" × 38½".

3 Referring to the quilt assembly diagram on page 80, join the block rows and sashing rows, alternating them as shown. The quilt top should measure 38½" × 52½", including seam allowances.

4 Join the remaining gold 1½" × 42" strips end to end. From the pieced strip, cut two 52½"-long strips. Sew the strips to the left and right sides of the quilt top. Sew the gold 40½"-long strips to the top and bottom edges. The quilt top should measure 40½" × 54½", including seam allowances.

5 Join the cream 3"-wide strips end to end. From the pieced strip, cut two 54½"-long strips and two 45½"-long strips. Sew the longer strips to the left and right sides of the quilt top. Sew the shorter strips to the top and bottom edges. The quilt top should measure 45½" × 59½", including seam allowances.

6 Join 30 cream and 29 assorted print 1½" squares to make a side border measuring 1½" × 59½", including seam allowances. Make two. Join 24 assorted print and 23 cream 1½" squares to

Designed, pieced, and quilted by Jessica Dayon.

Look for Jessica's quilts on Instagram @jessicadayon.

make a top border measuring 1½" × 47½", including seam allowances. Repeat to make the bottom border. Sew the longer strips to the left and right sides of the quilt top. Sew the shorter strips to the top and bottom edges. The quilt top should measure 47½" × 61½", including seam allowances.

Make 2 side borders,
1½" × 59½".

Make 2 top/bottom borders,
1½" × 47½".

7 Join the cream 2"-wide strips end to end. From the pieced strip, cut two 61½"-long strips and two 50½"-long strips. Sew the longer strips to the left and right sides of the quilt top. Sew the shorter strips to the top and bottom edges. The quilt top should measure 50½" × 64½", including seam allowances.

8 Join the green 3½"-wide strips end to end. From the pieced strip, cut two 64½"-long strips and two 56½"-long strips. Sew the longer strips to the left and right sides of the quilt top. Sew the shorter strips to the top and bottom edges. The quilt top should measure 56½" × 70½".

Finishing the Quilt

For more details on any finishing steps, visit ShopMartingale.com/HowtoQuilt for free downloadable information.

1 Layer the quilt top with batting and backing; baste the layers together.

2 Quilt by hand or machine. Jessica's quilt is machine quilted with an allover meander design.

3 Use the brown 2½"-wide strips to make double-fold binding. Attach the binding to the quilt.

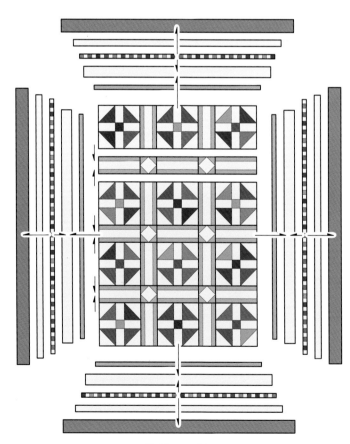

Quilt assembly

Charmed by Moda Bake Shop